Self-Esteem

An Instructional Manual For Overcoming Low Self-Esteem And Resolving Internal Conflicts To Restore Confidence

(Optimal Approaches For Attaining Success Through Practical Self-Sufficiency)

Emiliano Mancini

TABLE OF CONTENT

Is There An Equivalence Between Self-Esteem And Self-Confidence?..1

Comprehending The Level Of Self-Confidence..6

The Transformative Power Of Positive Affirmations In Shaping One's Life.....................19

A Demonstrative Endeavor Towards Optimism 26

Strategies Focused On Achieving Desired Outcomes In Enhancing Self-Esteem And Self-Confidence...36

Ensure Your Personal Well-Being Through The Practice Of Benevolence...45

Positivity And Self-Belief..55

The Beneficial Impact Of Goal Setting On Psychological Well-Being..79

Enhancing Self-Perception.....................................87

Effective Practices For Enhancing One's Self-Esteem...96

What Does This Book Contain And Who Should Engage With Its Contents?.................................115

Therapeutic Interventions And Psychosocial Support - Stage 2..120

Effective Strategies For Enhancing Positivity 130

Is There An Equivalence Between Self-Esteem And Self-Confidence?

Self-esteem and self-confidence are frequently employed as synonymous concepts. While similarities can be observed between the two concepts, it is important to recognize that each possesses distinct attributes and traits.

Self-esteem and Self-confidence defined

Self-esteem is a term utilized by psychologists to describe an individual's evaluation of their own worth or value. It is frequently linked to an individual's character, encompassing their conduct, sentiments, convictions, and physical presentation. It is commonly denoted as self-respect or self-esteem by others.

In contrast, self-assurance is a disposition which enables individuals to accurately and optimistically perceive themselves and their capabilities. It is associated with a positive outlook, self-assurance, warmth, autonomy, self-esteem, emotional development, and proficiency in handling critique in a constructive manner.

Self-esteem is intrinsically ingrained, encompassing an individual's entirety, while self-confidence has the capacity to extend over the entirety of a person or solely certain facets of their character. A gentleman who possesses assuredness regarding a matter may not necessarily harbor a considerable esteem for his own person. Let us examine the characteristics typically associated with the portrayal of athletic individuals commonly depicted in films. These individuals who are regarded as sports heroes are frequently portrayed as individuals who personify confidence in their performance on the field or court. In the realm of inter-personal relationships, it is notable that they exhibit tendencies to engage in bullying behavior and assert their self-worth onto others—a clear illustration of individuals who possess diminished levels of self-esteem. Similarly, individuals who are avid movie enthusiasts are often portrayed as being capable of effortlessly solving complex equations, yet they exhibit extreme introversion when faced with the task of articulately explaining their mathematical problem-solving process.

In both instances, individuals categorized as "nerds" and "jocks" demonstrate a sense of assurance in their respective fields of proficiency. However, they exhibit a deficiency in cultivating a mature mindset to comport themselves appropriately.

Men who possess confidence possess a precise evaluation of their capabilities and possess an innate belief in what the future holds. They possess a satisfactory level of autonomy that empowers them to pursue their objectives, aspirations, and intentions. They possess a practical mindset in life and demonstrate the ability to acknowledge that not all circumstances will align with their preferences. They are aware of their limitations as well as their capabilities. Individuals have the capacity to adopt a reflective stance and evaluate their circumstances in the event that things do not unfold according to their intended plans. Moreover, they possess the ability to perceive setbacks as valuable prospects for further refinement and development.

This mindset facilitates their willingness to acknowledge the inevitability of occasional failures or the inability to achieve all of their desired objectives. Hence, their ambition to achieve excellence in their pursuits is moderated by their acknowledgement of the potential for non-success.

Enhancing one's self-esteem has a similar effect on self-assurance, whereas a deficiency in self-esteem is manifested through a person's level of confidence. The way in which you assess your worth in terms of your work, accomplishments, social standing, and life's purpose has a direct connection to the level of confidence you exhibit. Frequently, individuals possessing diminished self-assurance exhibit an unfavorable perception of themselves while concurrently experiencing an overwhelming sense of inferiority. They do not perceive themselves to be devoid of praise, inconsequential, devoid of significance, and without love.

In the event that you experience feelings of timidity or social reclusiveness, it is imperative to discern whether your condition can be attributed to a lack of self-assurance or simply insufficient confidence to navigate social situations. In a practical scenario, this delineates the distinction between lacking direction (confidence) and lacking faith in one's own abilities (esteem).

Comprehending The Level Of Self-Confidence

You might be pondering how your present state of self-assurance has been shaped. There are a multitude of factors that impact this. Although it would be unjust to hold our parents entirely accountable for all the challenges we face in our present lives, it is generally during the phase of approximately two to three years old that we commence our journey towards fostering self-assurance. Following this, the influence of our parents significantly contributes to our present state of self-assurance. Children who receive affirmations regarding their inherent value and significance have a tendency to develop robust levels of self-esteem as they progress into adulthood.

Children whose parents exhibit a propensity towards excessive criticism and readily identify flaws or perceived failures are at an increased risk of facing challenges in their self-assurance. At present, it is not opportune to hold your parents accountable and harbor resentment towards them. Nevertheless, in the event that you are a parent, this piece of information should serve as a revelatory insight.

As individuals advance in age, social circles may also exert influence on their levels of self-assurance. Indeed, prior to hastily passing judgment upon your parents, it is crucial to acknowledge that there are instances in which peers wield a greater influence than one's parents. There is a rationale behind the counsel of wise individuals, urging one to exercise discernment when selecting companions. Children occasionally exhibit unkind behavior. In the event that your parental figures were not present to nurture your self-confidence and you subsequently found yourself in a peer group that also lacked encouragement, your self-assurance was unable to fully develop.

Adults typically possess a greater ability to recognize detrimental relationships, yet they often encounter challenges when determining appropriate courses of action, particularly when their self-assurance has been undermined. One must possess the self-assurance to communicate to a friend that their presence is detrimental to one's well-being. If he is unable to provide you with support or offer encouragement, it is imperative that he does not remain a part of your close-knit circle. In the course of cultivating your self-assurance, it is conceivable that you will need to undertake a process of selectively disassociating yourself from certain acquaintances. Please do not fret over your solitude, as we shall explore strategies in the subsequent chapters on forming meaningful connections with individuals who appreciate your true self.

Once you have eliminated the detrimental influences from your life, it will be necessary to embark upon the requisite measures to emancipate yourself from all the counterproductive and undesirable negative emotions. If you are prepared to commence the process of enhancing your self-esteem at this present moment, please continue reading.

In order to attain a specific objective in life, it is imperative for individuals to possess a requisite level of discipline, skills, aptitude, perseverance, and above all, self-assurance. This specific sense of assurance arises from the acquisition of appropriate skill sets, coupled with a precise understanding of the objectives to be accomplished. An individual's optimal functioning does not occur until their capabilities of both mind and body are complemented by a solid foundation of self-assurance. To disclose the truth, our self-esteem is the central point around which all aspects of the human intellect, both creative and analytical, depend. Due to this rationale, a deficiency in self-assurance has the capacity to significantly hinder the functioning of both the cognitive faculties and the physical well-being, consequently resulting in dire consequences.

In the realm of human existence, the attainment of remarkable accomplishments remains elusive unless one possesses a requisite measure of self-assurance. Insufficient self-assurance will impede progress, rendering one's exceptional skills and abilities insufficient in achieving success. This is due to the fact that diminished self-esteem possesses the capability to impede your progress in life, thereby rendering it unfeasible for you to undertake any form of proactive action. It seems to exert a paralyzing influence over both the cognitive and physical faculties when confronted with the task of making independent choices. It is imperative to bear in mind that in this existence, confidence bestows remarkable opportunities upon individuals, as it possesses the capacity to profoundly shape and determine one's journey unlike any other factor. Having a sense of self-assurance is paramount if you aspire to unleash the latent warrior residing within you.

It is imperative to acknowledge the fundamental reality that our self-confidence, alternatively known as self-esteem, possesses the capacity to exert influence over every facet of our existence. It is precisely that particular element that serves as the determinant of our achievements in life. The issue concerning self-confidence lies in its impact on one's emotional, cognitive, and occasionally physical well-being. The aforementioned outlook enables individuals to maintain optimistic and practical perspectives regarding not only their personal lives, but also towards any circumstances they come across. Nevertheless, possessing self-assurance does not guarantee the attainment of all life's endeavors. Rather, it endows individuals with the capacity to wholeheartedly devote themselves to every endeavor, unencumbered by doubt or hesitation regarding their abilities.

The unfortunate aspect pertaining to individuals who endure a dearth of self-assurance is their substantial reliance on the approbation bestowed upon them by others, dictating their decision-making, behavior, and potentially even their attire. They exert minimal influence over the course of their lives, often harboring doubts regarding the feasibility of attaining success. Despite being given a compliment, they tend to disregard or undervalue it due to their belief that they are unworthy of such praise. However, individuals often respond to compliments by undermining themselves through self-deprecating remarks, resulting in a diminished likelihood of receiving kind remarks in the future due to the negative response elicited. However, individuals who possess self-assurance exhibit a propensity to resist external influence, as they possess unwavering belief in their own capabilities. Such individuals possess a strong sense of self-awareness, embracing their identity and valuing themselves enough to resist societal pressures to conform simply for acceptance.

Indeed, the bedrock of self-assurance is rooted in a profound sense of self-acceptance and self-love, embracing both our strengths and weaknesses. You perceive yourself through the lens of optimistic pragmatism and self-esteem that arises from living genuinely, in accordance with your principles and within the boundaries of your values. An individual possessing self-assurance comprehends their true self, their preferred way of life, and adeptly transcends setbacks and errors, following a suitable duration of sorrow and introspection.

One's level of self-confidence does not hinge upon being a top achiever, attaining financial success, possessing remarkable physical attractiveness, or exhibiting exceptional intelligence. Indeed, even individuals of average stature and ordinariness are capable of possessing copious amounts of self-assurance. While it is true that certain individuals may inherit a genetic inclination towards a favorable outlook or appealing physical features, it is important to acknowledge that genetic makeup does not solely determine one's traits. Acquiring and cultivating faith is an attainable endeavor, one that can be developed through the acquisition of specific aptitudes conducive to building trust. With the possession of these skills, individuals possess the ability to actively shape their lives instead of merely responding to its circumstances. You possess authority over your own fate, and the sole obstacle blocking your path is your perception of yourself—and conceivably an insufficiency of understanding regarding how to modify your thoughts and emotions.

Self-awareness is integral to the development of confidence. You have conducted a thorough self-assessment, resulting in a firm conviction regarding your priorities, desired lifestyle, and personal identity. A life that has been subjected to thorough examination provides a structure that instills confidence by offering security and setting clear boundaries. When one finds oneself struggling in life, beset by uncertainty regarding appropriate conduct or courses of action, one experiences a state of apprehension and bewilderment. In the absence of guidance or a set of guiding principles, it becomes challenging to experience a sense of self-assurance.

Confidence does not necessitate consistently being at the peak of your performance, constantly assertive and in control, yet maintaining a refined and cultivated demeanor. It does not necessitate fearlessness in all circumstances, nor does it imply the requirement to possess extroverted qualities or excel in public speaking. Fundamentally, genuine confidence entails wholeheartedly accepting one's authentic identity and cultivating self-affection, all the while persistently striving for personal growth. It pertains to establishing a framework for your operations, grounded in your fundamental principles and ethical standards, and subsequently shaping your life in accordance with this framework.

Kindly be aware that if you currently lack self-confidence, there is potential for growth and development should you be amenable to implementing certain modifications. This process will necessitate introspection, paradigm shifts, and behavioral modifications. It will necessitate disciplined effort and perseverance, for substantial achievements require such commitment. Enhancing your confidence necessitates cultivating a substantial level of self-esteem, characterized by an ample supply of affirmative emotions regarding your fundamental value, enabling you to embrace self-acceptance and appreciate the wisdom and discernment within yourself.

Numerous individuals possess a perplexing perception, considering self-esteem and self-confidence as interchangeable terms representing a singular notion. While they may share a close relationship and rely on each other, it should be noted that they are not identical. As previously stated, confidence refers to having trust in one's capabilities and discernment. Fundamentally, it signifies that you harbor a conviction in your proactive abilities, self-sufficiency, and perseverance. Self-esteem embodies an individual's comprehensive evaluation of their inherent value. Your self-esteem is predicated upon one's perception of their intrinsic worth as an individual, coupled with the emotional outlook assigned to these convictions. It is entirely possible to experience a shortage of confidence while retaining a healthy level of self-esteem. It is significantly more challenging to grapple with a lack of self-esteem while endeavoring to maintain a sense of confidence in oneself and one's capabilities.

The Transformative Power Of Positive Affirmations In Shaping One's Life

Cultivating a positive mindset is instrumental in attaining happiness and achieving a prosperous existence. Our mental disposition plays a pivotal role in shaping our life's trajectory.

Considerations play a significant role in influencing our emotions and promoting optimistic thinking.

Instills a positive outlook in an individual's daily life, whereas negativity leads to a decrease in confidence.

It is remarkable how much you have missed out on in life. We so frequently work

We often deceive ourselves without recognizing the act, commonly resulting in multiple negative consequences.

Various contemplations traverse our consciousness as we engage in excessive self-criticism.

and instill a sense of doubt. There exists a limited set of fundamental equipment that you can employ.

Throughout the course of the day, make a concerted effort to replace these negative thoughts and cultivate a more positive mindset.

Approaching situations from an optimistic standpoint and integrating daily affirmations of positivity can enhance the quality of one's life.

definitely. They have the potential to enhance your confidence, heighten your awareness, bolster your self-assurance, and positively transform various aspects of your life.

What are positive affirmations?

Positive affirmations can be employed throughout the day, regardless of location or time.

The more frequently you employ them, the more positive thoughts will gradually replace negative ones.

By incorporating positive habits, you will experience tangible benefits in your life. An assertion is a fundamental approach.

This technique is employed to transform our occasional unconscious negative self-talk into a more positive outlook on life. The

The majority of us have long surrounded ourselves with pessimistic thoughts, therefore altering your mindset would be beneficial.

"Deliberations and the manner in which you contemplate will not happen fortuitously but rather, if by chance

It is imperative that you adhere to the requirement of obtaining certifications, as they will prove beneficial once you have successfully retrained your perspective. There

There are numerous procedures available to manage various circumstances in everyday life, and the following list highlights the most popular and effective options.

The mirror technique

This approach promotes the act of embracing oneself and cultivating a state of self-awareness and assurance.

It is advisable for you to stand in front of a mirror, preferably a full-length one, wearing only your clothing or undergarments.

ter still stripped. Commencing from the superior region of your body, articulate audibly the comprehensive description of each component as you progress inferiorly.

Do you have any preferences regarding specific areas of your body? For instance, you could express your appreciation for the way in which your hair sparkles, the slight contrasts in shading where the light hits it" or " my eyes are a beautiful

Nuance of _ _. The objects exude a radiance and brilliance, captivating my vision as an extraordinary element. Please allocate the necessary resources to observe them thoroughly.

Furthermore, progressively cultivate a comprehensive perception of yourself as you engage in your workout regimen.

The anywhere technique

This technique can be employed in any location and at any time that you find yourself contemplating a situation.

When a negative notion arises, it is advisable to actively disengage from it and mentally redirect your focus.

"Adjust the volume control within your mind to lower it to a suitable level so as to avoid

to listen to it any longer. At that juncture, consider affirming in a constructive manner to replace the negative notion and subsequently amplify the intensity, repeating it inwardly.

The trash can technique

If you happen to have any unfavorable thoughts, kindly jot them down on a sheet of paper.

Crumple the paper into a ball and discard it in the waste bin; through this action, you acknowledge that these thoughts are merely frivolous and have no relevance.

The meditation technique

Seek out a tranquil setting in which you can embark on a brief period of relaxation, by closing your eyes for approximately 5 to 10 minutes.

Exercise impartiality and suppress emotional influences within your mind. Commence the process of revisiting and reinforcing your declaration to yourself.

Continuously reaffirm oneself, with unwavering attention on the statements being reiterated, and have faith in the veracity of one's words.

A Demonstrative Endeavor Towards Optimism

I request that you make an effort to compile a list. This task might prove challenging if you possess a pessimistic outlook regarding your skills; however, it is within the realm of possibility for individuals of all abilities. Thus, it is crucial to exhibit patience with oneself throughout this process. The enumeration will encompass all the elements that bring you pleasure and contentment in your existence. These will be tasks that you possess knowledge about, are capable of doing, and feel at ease performing. In the event that you encounter any challenges with this task, kindly take a moment to shut your eyes and reflect upon instances in your past wherein you experienced feelings of joy and contentment. Through a meticulous analysis, one shall ascertain the causal factors that engendered sensations of happiness and confidence within oneself. As an illustration, you may recall a specific instance where you experienced an immense sense of self-satisfaction. The perpetrator's identity or motive is inconsequential. Please endeavor to recollect that sensation and create a record of the aspects that evoked a sense of transcendence within you.

We will not be lingering on the negative feelings you hold towards yourself, as you have already dwelled upon them extensively. At present, you are experiencing a pivotal moment in your life whereby it becomes imperative to compile a catalogue of positive aspects to reflect upon whenever confronted with individuals or circumstances that tend to undermine your self-esteem. I can recall a specific incident from my early years when I donned an exceptional ensemble and received admiration for my appearance. Certainly, I am more than capable of undertaking that task presently. However, it is often overlooked by individuals who navigate through life burdened by pessimism and low self-regard, that there exist numerous instances in which they exhibited remarkable abilities or achieved great success. This holds true for every individual. Irrespective of the simplicity of your thoughts, it is imperative that you inscribe them, as they hold considerable value to your existence.

A demonstration of self-assurance.

In this exercise, I am requesting for you to examine your body's alignment. Take a look in the mirror and if you have a full length mirror, place it so that you can see yourself enter a room. A lack of self-confidence becomes evident through one's gait and demeanor, both of which reflect how they interact with and perceive the surrounding environment. Your head may be inclined at a more pronounced angle than usual. You may exhibit a slight tendency to hunch your shoulders and fidget with your hands while engaging in conversation with others. Today, I kindly request that you rectify your posture. It is imperative that you maintain forward gaze of the head. It is imperative that you maintain proper posture, ensuring that your shoulders are aligned in a straight manner. Should you have a tendency to slump or slouch, it is important to be acutely aware of the fact that this posture diminishes your perceived presence and stature. Your countenance also reveals your true intentions. If one is unable to establish direct eye contact and convey a pleasant facial expression, it can create the perception of lacking self-assurance and potentially harboring personal concerns. Engage in mirror practice, followed by confidently adopting the recommended posture and cultivating a pleasant countenance as you interact with the individuals encountered while strolling down the street.

Self-assurance is also evident in the manner in which one articulates oneself. Certain individuals encounter difficulty when it comes to engaging in verbal communication with others, which leads me to request that you make an audio recording of your voice. Perform this task within the confines of your personal dwelling, specifically within the seclusion of your room, while first presenting yourself and subsequently acquainting yourself with the audio representation. Individuals can acquire highly indolent behaviors and exhibit a lack of articulate speech. Let's try it again. On this occasion, assume the persona of a renowned actor and proceed to reintroduce yourself. By assuming an additional role, you are effectively equipping yourself to articulate in a manner consistent with that of the actor. Please make another attempt, this time envisioning that you are communicating with your superior, while maintaining a position of equal significance. Individuals who exhibit a deficit in self-assurance often demonstrate tendencies of submissiveness, which can consequently lead to various predicaments. Envision yourself as an educator imparting knowledge to a cohort of students with regards to the fundamentals of phonetic symbols encompassing the alphabet. Please reiterate the lesson on your recording device while considering an audience comprising of children who face challenges in grasping concepts. It is imperative that you enunciate your words with absolute clarity, leaving no room for ambiguity in your communication. Practice it again. Perform the task repeatedly until you reach a state of contentment and open-mindedness towards the auditory perception presented during the playback of the recording.

Prior to concluding the recording, I kindly request you to earnestly capture these sentences, as they shall serve as an enduring reminder for you that your significance is equal to that of every other individual.

I am an individual of substantial value, deserving of one's acquaintance. I possess a welcoming and amicable demeanor, and I harbor no hesitation about engaging with individuals."

Now, moving on to the subsequent segment of the exercise, I aim to evaluate your aptitude for offering without soliciting any form of reciprocation. It is evident that individuals who are in need or possess low self-confidence often exhibit a strong inclination towards seeking excessive validation. You may seek your supervisor's validation regarding your performance, which distinguishes you from individuals who are content with fulfilling their responsibilities. Seeking validation from others may decrease your chances of receiving a promotion. It indicates a deficiency in self-assurance and an excessive reliance on external validation, which creates unfavorable dynamics for those in your social vicinity as individuals seeking constant affirmation can be mentally and emotionally draining on others. In the pursuit of various endeavors, it is crucial to develop the ability to undertake them for personal growth and fulfillment rather than solely to seek approval or validation from others. The opinions of others hold little significance as long as your own satisfaction with your actions remains intact. The sheer delight and self-assurance derived from abstaining to anticipate any form of recompense is truly remarkable. Thus, select an assignment that you are capable of undertaking on behalf of a companion or a resident in your vicinity. You may consider the possibility of preparing a cake for an elderly resident in your neighborhood, or alternatively, offering your services as a volunteer to take dogs for a walk at the nearby animal shelter. I kindly request your compliance in this matter, as it is essential to recognize that personal fulfillment stems from one's own recognition of one's own endeavours, rather than seeking external validation. Execute the task without any expectations. Don't expect praise. Please refrain from engaging in self-aggrandizement regarding your accomplishments. Do it with the primary intention of experiencing positive emotions, and the desired outcome shall surely be realized.

The objective of these exercises is to endeavor towards enhancing one's perception of oneself. Voluntary engagement facilitates the attainment of that objective; nevertheless, one should volunteer with an absence of expectations regarding visibility or recognition. This introduces a notion of necessity, and presently, the sole necessity you have is to experience personal satisfaction regarding an action you undertake.

Strategies Focused On Achieving Desired Outcomes In Enhancing Self-Esteem And Self-Confidence

As demonstrated previously in the literature, we were introduced to the significance of possessing optimal self-esteem and self-assurance in an individual's existence. Similarly, it is evident that the interplay of these two factors holds significant influence over the extent of accomplishment. For this reason, this section aims to reveal diverse methods through which you can elevate both your self-esteem and self-confidence. Additionally, owing to the significant resemblance between these two elements, the below enhancement option will effectively elevate both factors.

"Now, let us proceed:

Manifesting a resilient and determined attitude is an indispensable trait for any trailblazer. It signifies that one must possess self-confidence in their ability to attain certain objectives. In accordance with the commonly held axiom, if one does not take initiative in assisting oneself, external help becomes an impossibility. This does not signify that nobody will make an effort to assist you in various manners; they indeed would. However, the desired change ultimately depends on the personal actions that you will undertake. A considerable number of accomplished individuals have encountered numerous obstacles on their journey towards their current position. The distinguishing factor lies in their ability to embrace a steadfast mindset that is characterized by unwavering determination and confidence, ensuring that regardless of the obstacles they encounter, they will confront them head-on and achieve their objective.

Enhance personal capabilities (Self-improvement): Insufficient readiness has also been identified as a notable factor contributing to diminished levels of self-assurance and self-esteem. Given the aforementioned circumstances, it is imperative that you take all necessary measures to maintain your personal appearance. Will you be attending a presentation, examination, tutoring session, or deliberation? By proactively acquiring pertinent knowledge in advance, you will undoubtedly elevate your levels of self-assurance and self-worth beyond what you anticipate.

Gain self-awareness regarding your strengths and weaknesses: One error that individuals often make is presuming that every trailblazer possesses flawless perfection in every aspect. Contrary to any preconceptions, it is important to acknowledge that even individuals who significantly alter the course of world affairs possess vulnerabilities that are, in fact, deeply ingrained within their character. However, what sets them apart is their ability to recognize and capitalize on their strengths in order to distinguish themselves from the competition. Therefore, it is imperative to pause and thoroughly reflect in order to discern your areas of strength, subsequently utilizing them to enact the desired transformation. Regardless, every weakness can be improved upon. In addition to capitalizing on your strengths, dedicating attention to your weaknesses and transforming them into advantages will significantly enhance your self-esteem and confidence.

Eliminate pessimistic thoughts from your consciousness: Negativity, if not addressed diligently, has the potential to impede success even when one possesses the utmost capability to triumph. Negativity holds considerable influence in diminishing an individual's self-esteem and confidence. Yet, you possess the means to render its impact ineffectual in your life. And the crucial aspect lies in the act of counteracting negative thoughts by introducing positive thoughts.

Consider your accomplishments: There exist particular instances or experiences in life that may cause us to feel apprehensive, probing our inner thoughts, or questioning our ability to surmount obstacles. At this juncture, if precautions are not taken, the rapid influx of unfavorable thoughts within one's mind could potentially have an adverse impact on an individual's level of confidence and self-worth. However, a prompt and alternative approach to mitigating the negative impact is to reflect upon the past accomplishments that you have attained. This serves to instill in you the belief that successful attainment of a particular objective in the past indisputably equips you with the ability to surmount the impending challenge.

Exercise caution and moderation when engaging in communication with others. It is worth noting that some individuals may perceive the deliberate adjustment of one's speaking pace as an effective means to enhance their self-assurance and assertiveness. It is evident that the manner in which you conduct your conversation significantly dictates the degree of recognition you garner from your listeners. Certain individuals possess extensive knowledge on the matter at hand; however, the rapidity at which they convey their thoughts, stemming from the swift flow of ideas in their mind, may impede their ability to articulate their point effectively. Consequently, their confidence and self-esteem may suffer, particularly due to the inability to meet the expectations surrounding the discourse or presentation. Do you not believe that adopting a gradual and measured approach in unveiling your speeches would engender a heightened propensity for audience attentiveness?

If you tend to encounter challenges in effectively conveying verbal information to others, it would be highly beneficial for you to adopt a slower pace. This will enhance individuals' receptiveness to your message, thereby bolstering your motivation and contributing to a more enriching experience. Hence, it is crucial to recognize that the deliberate pace at which you convey your ideas does not diminish your ability to effectively influence your audience.

Encountering a hurdle is a prerequisite for individuals who aspire to achieve success.

There remains a prevalent belief among numerous individuals that challenges should be entirely avoided. Do you belong to this particular group of individuals? The reality lies in the notion that, in the absence of life's trials, we will persist in our current state and potentially experience further deterioration. The obstacle that one must overcome with success in order to not only progress to the next stage of life, but also reach higher levels of achievement, is referred to as a challenge. Consider an individual who is hesitant to undertake a promotional examination out of apprehension for the possibility of failure. Consider envisioning a person who possesses a disinclination towards employment yet has an aspiration to generate a consistent and enduring source of income. What about an athlete who incessantly harbors aspirations of triumph but lacks the inclination to undertake the arduous trials of rigorous training? The fundamental principle at play is that obstacles serve as catalysts for personal and collective growth, propelling individuals to ascend to higher levels of achievement. In addition to adapting to these challenges, you are also cultivating self-esteem and confidence, equipping you with the ability to tackle future obstacles.

In addition to the aforementioned suggestions for enhancing your self-esteem and confidence, the following recommendations will prove beneficial and should be incorporated into your personal guidelines:

The imperative to perceive change as an enduring component of life and remain perpetually prepared for its inevitability.

Exert efforts to generate effective resolutions for the requirements of individuals in your vicinity.

Consistently displaying friendly behaviors such as smiling and responding to greetings, among other similar gestures.

Express gratitude towards the individuals in your vicinity.

keep yourself physically fit.

manage your time well.

refrain from being idle

Make gradual progress towards your desired objectives; a measured and consistent approach has the capacity to emerge victorious in the competition.

don't procrastinate.

Acquiring knowledge provides individuals with a pathway to attain power. Given the comprehensive array of tools at your disposal, it becomes imperative to incorporate an additional element – namely, discipline. This encourages adherence to your predetermined course of action, regardless of the circumstances. Finally, it is imperative that you never allow yourself to lose motivation.

Ensure Your Personal Well-Being Through The Practice Of Benevolence.

In order to circumvent emotional manipulation, it is imperative that you cultivate the ability to engage in impartial thinking. The concept of neutral thinking distinguishes itself by preventing us from becoming entangled in various experiences and thoughts that might otherwise occur without its presence. Developing the ability to objectively assess ourselves may require some dedicated effort. Once you acquire the ability to engage in objective thinking, you will increasingly discern your thoughts, emotions, and actions without resorting to judgment. This will undoubtedly assist you in the pursuit of your path to self-actualization.

To advance as individuals, it is imperative that we comprehend that our thoughts do not define our true nature. One's thoughts do not define one's identity. They fail to exemplify your personal identity. They are independent of you. Ideas are not subject to deliberate cultivation; rather, they arise spontaneously, and one must acquire the skill to navigate them. This necessitates assuming a passive role and observing the contents of your mind as one would observe a television program. Observe the contents being displayed on the television screen as it cycles through channels automatically. It will traverse the distance between these two points, spanning from the past to the future. The mind will be prone to wander, presenting various scenarios for contemplation. Subsequently, it is within your discretion to determine where your attention is directed. You will observe the emergence of a thought. One can develop the skill of recognizing this thought by observing its entrance into their consciousness as if peering through a window, gently drifting, and subsequently departing through the same window, thereby permeating their consciousness. This imagery can aid in the realization that one's thoughts exist autonomously, detached from the self, and that they reside in an ethereal domain, devoid of actuality. Such is a realization that eludes the majority: thoughts lacks inherent reality.

Upon careful reflection of its intricate nature, it becomes evident that one's thoughts are a highly abstract notion. It is the process by which we employ language that we have acquired in order to spontaneously generate ideas in our minds and articulate them internally, using our own voice, but without any external audience. It is something that you can certainly dedicate time to exploring if it interests you. Take a moment to reflect upon the marvel that is consciousness.

Cognition fundamentally pertains to the consciousness of human beings, distinct from the conscious experiences of animals. The human form can be considered the most remarkable instrument known to us in the vast expanse of the cosmos. The capacity of the human intellect is so immensely profound that it has given rise to societies characterized by the manifestations of extraordinary benevolence and extraordinarily destructive malevolence. The human mind cannot be measured or quantified in any way; it solely exists in the realm of abstraction. There are specific approaches available to quantify behavior or brain chemicals, as well as certain components of brain function. Nevertheless, it remains infeasible for any individual to truly comprehend the subjective experiences of another. They have the ability to provide a description to you, however, as we will later elaborate, language serves as a rudimentary instrument and may not invariably convey precision. The basic distinction cannot be fully encompassed by any amount of descriptions or quantification. The notion of division is intrinsic to our human nature and compels the pursuit of individuality.

Section 4.1: Comprehensive Instructions for Enhancing Listening Skills

The cultivation of effective listening abilities is a highly valuable asset when it comes to enhancing emotional intelligence. When discussing emotional intelligence, we are referring to the capacity to comprehend and empathize with others. What better offering can there be to cultivate comprehension of others than attentive listening? The skill of attentive listening affords us an invaluable insight into the lives of others, and possessing such insight bestows upon us a profound obligation, coupled with a distinct honor. It is imperative to exhibit proper regard for others and refrain from exploiting the authority bestowed upon oneself as an effective listener. You are required to consistently demonstrate good faith while exercising this authority.

An individual who possesses the quality of being an attentive listener has the ability to navigate a complete discourse with minimal verbal contributions or inquiries. They possess the capacity to steer discussions without verbal communication through the modification of their nonverbal cues. It is possible that they are completely engrossed in the act of listening, rendering any inclination to speak unnecessary. The degree to which this may vary is contingent upon the subject matter one wishes to discuss and the urgency with which they feel compelled to do so.

Enhancing one's ability to actively listen can significantly impact their effectiveness as a communicator, distinguishing them between being a subpar communicator and an adept one. An effective communicator possesses the ability to encapsulate and articulate the entirety of the other party's remarks. An individual proficient in effective communication will demonstrate excellent listening skills as they possess the ability to carefully and attentively assimilate information. Effective communication is contingent upon the exchange of verbal expressions between two individuals. In order to foster effective communication, it is necessary to establish a reciprocal feedback mechanism between two entities.

Listening skills involve experiencing a particular emotional disposition towards an individual. Are you able to recall an instance in which you experienced a sense of being embraced and cherished? It could potentially be a parent, a schoolteacher, a counselor, or another individual. This is an ability that is exemplified by a truly exceptional listener. They have the potential to elicit feelings of intellect. They have the capacity to create a sense of active involvement and meaningful interaction, ensuring that you feel adequately included and treated fairly. Individuals have a natural inclination to receive acknowledgment and recognition, hence by affording them your attention alone, you can bestow upon them a surprisingly substantial level of validation.

Having the capacity to undertake such tasks for individuals is undeniably an invaluable aptitude in the realm of artistry. The majority of therapists undertake the acquisition of this skill, enabling them to become adept at assuming the role of impartial observers to any given situation. When an individual is aware that they are being heard by others, they experience a sense of their own significance within the world, along with an acknowledgment of the profound influence they can exert. Indeed, a considerable number of individuals seeking therapy for different purposes erroneously believe they possess a crucial necessity for therapeutic intervention, failing to recognize their underlying requirements for acknowledgment, affection, and the experience of being heard by others. Individuals may engage in therapy without fully recognizing the underlying dynamic, and over the course of multiple sessions, provided that the therapist is proficient, they will gradually experience improvements in their emotional well-being through the process of expressing their thoughts and feelings. Certain individuals have a deep longing to be heard, yet regrettably, their voices often go unheard.

Expressing one's needs can be challenging, and it can occasionally be beneficial to seek the attentive ear of others. On certain occasions, it becomes necessary to seek the assistance of an expert in order to make progress.

Ultimately, the cultivation of effective listening skills necessitates an individual's genuine curiosity concerning the world and their fellow beings. It is imperative that you possess a genuine interest in understanding the underlying motivations behind human behavior, coupled with a sincere inclination towards spreading happiness among individuals. The state of "beginner's mind" is characterized by childlike fascination with each new experience, and it is this mindset that we ought to endeavor to cultivate. One should appreciate and embrace the diverse qualities that distinguish us as individuals, and eagerly welcome the chance to cultivate empathy towards those who possess dissimilarities.

Positivity And Self-Belief

In the introductory section, we have briefly discussed the fundamental elements of self-esteem and the significance it carries. Furthermore, within the confines of this chapter, we shall integrate the subject matter pertaining to the acquisition of self-assurance. Self-assurance is frequently misconstrued with self-regard due to their apparent similarity, yet they are fundamentally disparate in meaning. The definition of self-confidence, as outlined in the Oxford dictionary, pertains to an individual's unwavering belief in their own capabilities, attributes, and discernment. Distinguished from self-esteem, self-confidence primarily revolves around one's performance, serving as a catalyst to bolster their assurance in persisting with their endeavors or embarking upon novel undertakings. When an individual possesses heightened self-assurance in their aptitude to carry out tasks, they are inclined to experience increased happiness as a result of a greater frequency of accomplishments. When an individual possesses faith in their own capacities, they are driven to undertake the necessary actions essential for the attainment of their objectives. Self-assurance primarily revolves around an individual's positive perception of their past achievements, thereby instilling the capability to enhance forthcoming endeavors.

Similar to self-esteem, self-confidence can be a challenging concept to grasp completely. It is crucial that we establish a precise understanding of the concept of self-confidence before proceeding any further, given its frequent utilization within the contents of this book. Presented herein are several illustrations that will enhance the elucidation of the meaning of self-confidence:

• An individual has the ability to recognize and appreciate their inherent worth, irrespective of any previous errors or missteps.

A person can still maintain a positive self-perception despite their flaws and consistently recognize their inherent worth.

• An individual possesses the courage to advocate for themselves and exhibit assertiveness.

• An individual is aware of their inherent worthiness to receive friendship and respect from others.

• An individual possesses comprehensive self-awareness and demonstrates the ability to embrace all aspects of their character, encompassing both their virtues and limitations.

Self-confidence does not encompass the following attributes:

- An individual holding a belief in their own perfection or a belief in the necessity or obligation to attain perfection.

- An individual who adheres to impractical standards and expectations

- An individual who aspires to lead a life devoid of hardships, afflictions, and difficulties.

- An individual exhibiting egocentrism and solely prioritizing their personal objectives and desires.

When individuals are initially acquainting themselves with the concept of self-confidence, it is not uncommon for them to conflate it with tunnel vision, characterized by a limited scope of concern solely centered on personal betterment, aiming to attain a more effortless and streamlined existence. While it remains a veracity that possessing self-assurance equips individuals with the necessary skills to handle the challenges life may present, it does not imply an everlasting shield against all problems. Moreover, there exists a widespread misconception among individuals that a fundamental aspect of cultivating self-assurance is solely centred on honing their own abilities and pursuing personal objectives. Nonetheless, it could be argued that such behavior is indicative of self-centeredness. Individuals who possess true self-assurance can be characterized as having unwavering faith in their personal identity and their ability to positively impact themselves and others. The aforementioned conduct enhances the likelihood for the individual to engage and establish connections with fellow individuals. Therefore, this enables individuals to establish a lifestyle that is characterized by improved equilibrium and enhanced well-being.

Having acquired an understanding of the concept of self-confidence, let us now delve into its application within the practical realm. Self-assurance operates by facilitating the attainment of optimal levels of self-regard, while fostering a sense of self-reliance. When an individual possesses a profound sense of self-assurance in their aptitude to achieve objectives, it is only natural that they will invariably experience a greater degree of success. Upon attaining this success, they shall acquire the necessary self-assurance to sustain their motivation in accomplishing further objectives. While self-esteem and self-confidence possess distinct characteristics, their collaboration facilitates the development of a positive self-relationship.

Let us delve into the various distinctions between self-esteem and self-confidence. As previously acknowledged, self-esteem pertains to an individual's self-perception and the extent of their self-compassion. An individual's self-esteem is constructed upon the accumulation of experiences and circumstances within their life, influencing their daily self-perception. Self-assurance refers to an individual's perception and emotional state regarding their own capabilities, which may vary depending on the circumstances at hand. As an illustration, an individual may possess a robust sense of self-worth, yet experience diminished self-assurance concerning their aptitude for social interactions. When individuals develop a strong sense of self-love, it fosters a notable enhancement in their self-esteem, subsequently instilling them with greater self-assurance and propelling them towards the pursuit of novel endeavors. As an individual's confidence gradually develops across various domains of their life, their overall self-esteem will progressively expand. Self-esteem and self-confidence synergistically collaborate. Hence, when an individual enhances their self-esteem, they concurrently elevate their self-confidence.

Allow us to acquire some knowledge regarding the shared qualities inherent in self-esteem and self-confidence. The primary commonality they possess is the capacity for self-love. Individuals who were raised in an environment characterized by a lack of appreciation from others frequently encounter difficulties in this regard, as their early experiences did not afford them the chance to cultivate self-worth. When an individual lacks a sense of being esteemed during their formative years, their self-esteem will diminish. In the event of disbelief in their own abilities or in themselves, individuals will experience a deficiency in their self-assurance. In a similar vein to the correlation between possessing self-esteem and acquiring self-confidence, a deficiency in self-esteem frequently results in a dearth of self-confidence.

In conclusion, it can be stated that self-esteem is the outcome of an individual's life experiences and the subsequent impact they have had on their sense of self. Self-assurance is the attribute whereby an individual perceives inherent worth in their abilities and actions. These two concepts, when combined, establish a consequential alliance that greatly shapes an individual's self-perception, ascertain their degree of assertiveness, and ultimately determine their overall level of self-assurance. Please peruse the ensuing suggestions to initiate the enhancement of your self-esteem and self-confidence.

• Make an effort to recall the positive attributes that others frequently commend you for. Irrespective of your personal belief regarding their veracity, kindly remind yourself of them. This marks the initial progress in the correct path.

• Endeavor to subdue the detrimental internal dialogue within your own cognition. Endeavor to consider alternative approaches that you may employ to refute or challenge the aforementioned remarks.

• In case you are experiencing detrimental self-perceptions, consider whether you would utter such statements to a cherished individual. If that is not the case, endeavor to abstain from entertaining such thoughts.

• Compile a roster of your areas of proficiency. Envision the statements you would articulate to yourself in the context of a professional job interview.

Factors contributing to diminished self-esteem

Individuals who experience low self-esteem frequently harbor negative perceptions of their own self and often experience feelings of inadequacy in comparison to others. Consequently, individuals belonging to this group face an elevated likelihood of being unable to actualize their full capabilities. Due to their lack of proactive engagement in establishing and striving for personal objectives, they may inadvertently allocate insufficient dedication towards critical endeavors, such as education and career advancement. They frequently exhibit a greater susceptibility to tolerating unfavorable treatment from individuals in their social circle, including friends, family members, and romantic partners. The investigation has indicated that these detrimental behaviors exhibit a correlation with diminished self-worth among teenagers and youth.

- Delinquency - Illicit conduct - Unlawful behavior - Antisocial acts - Violation of the law

• Adolescent pregnancy

• Withdrawing from educational institution

"● Inadequate scholastic achievement "● Subpar scholarly results "● Insufficient educational attainment "● Below-average marks or grades "● Lackluster academic progress

● Substance misuse and substance addiction

● Eating disorders

● Premature engagement in sexual behavior ● Premature initiation of sexual activity

The phenomenon of possessing low self-esteem encompasses a level of complexity that surpasses a mere negative emotional experience. Low self-esteem detrimentally impacts individuals' lives to a significant extent. Despite the challenges in ascertaining the prevalence of low self-esteem, numerous scientific investigations have yielded compelling findings indicating a notable decline in self-esteem levels among individuals on the brink of adolescence. Individuals within this demographic frequently develop a perception that they lack adequacy across multiple dimensions, such as interpersonal connections, physical attractiveness, and academic attainment.

If individuals develop low self-esteem during their early years, there is an increased likelihood that this condition will persist into their adult lives. This is where it starts to impede significant matters such as an individual's capacity to lead a gratifying and well-being-oriented existence. A crucial element regarding self-esteem is its divergence from an objective representation of reality, and its inherent variability. The underlying factors contributing to self-esteem can often be identified, yet it is misleading to hold onto the notion that one's self-perception is unalterable.

One's self-esteem is a cognitive framework that is inherently malleable.

An individual possessing robust self-esteem has the potential to experience a decline, resulting in diminished levels of self-confidence. Conversely, they also possess the capability to undergo positive transformations, leading to a substantial improvement in self-esteem. An individual can solely enhance their self-esteem through a willingness to recognize and commence the task of confronting their self-inflicted critical evaluations. Irrespective of the level of conviction an individual holds regarding their present self-assessment, embracing the potential capacity to regulate one's self-esteem presents only advantages and no disadvantages. Through the deliberate act of questioning their own thoughts, individuals can initiate a transformative process that alters both their cognitive patterns and their subsequent decision-making in the immediate and forthcoming periods. The following are examples of frequently observed factors contributing to diminished self-esteem in individuals. By considering this information, you may be able to recognize the possible origins within your own life that could be impacting your sense of self-worth.

Parents who exhibit a lack of engagement or fail to fulfill their responsibilities adequately

Virtually everyone, particularly during their formative years, experiences emotions regarding their self-perception, which are significantly influenced by the interactions with their immediate social circle during this period. This holds especially true in the case of their parents or guardians. Undoubtedly, it is an inherent right of every individual to have a nurturing family environment. Regrettably, certain individuals have been deprived of the essential care and affection that is imperative for the well-being of all. In these instances, it is common for parents to experience mental health challenges or comparable circumstances, resulting in an inability to adequately nurture their children and provide them with the requisite attention and guidance they both require and deserve. This leads to significant issues with self-esteem in individuals during their formative years, as those entrusted with their care are failing to fulfill their responsibilities adequately.

Negative Peers

In a manner akin to how individuals with diminished self-confidence frequently experienced significant impacts from the treatment of their parents or guardians, the influence of their peers during their formative years similarly holds great sway. If an individual is affiliated with a social collective that consistently undermines and disregards their worth, fails to appreciate their perspectives and emotions, or coerces them into engaging in activities that elicit discomfort, it can engender a sense of self-doubt and inadequacy within them. This imparts the notion that the sole means for gaining acceptance from others is to comply with their every desire, disregarding entirely their own thoughts and viewpoints. This has the potential to significantly undermine an individual's self-confidence.

Trauma

When an individual undergoes instances of physical, emotional, or sexual abuse, it frequently engenders sentiments of shame and guilt within the affected individual. The person in question might erroneously believe that their actions led to the mistreatment or that they lack the value and deservingness of the abuser's care, affection, and regard. Those who have experienced abuse may suffer from heightened levels of anxiety and depression, impeding their capacity to lead a contented and meaningful existence.

Body Image

According to recent scientific findings, researchers have discovered that approximately half of adolescent females express dissatisfaction with their body image. Moreover, this percentage escalates to nearly 80% once they reach the age of 17. In a comparable study, it was discovered that approximately 30% of adolescent males and 50% of adolescent females frequently engaged in detrimental behaviors with the aim of altering their weight to attain their desired physical appearance. These behaviors encompassed smoking tobacco, abstaining from meals, inducing vomiting, employing laxatives, and refraining from food consumption.

Body image significantly influences the self-esteem of young individuals, particularly among females. Since their birth, women have been consistently exposed to unattainable depictions of female beauty and societal standards dictating the ideal and desirable body types. This has led to the objectification of women's bodies in the media, perpetuating the notion that their physical forms solely exist for the pleasure, consumption, and exploitation of others. When the onset of puberty occurs and a young girl's body undergoes natural changes that differ from the idealized representations depicted in media, it frequently results in a sense of powerlessness and diminished self-perception in terms of attractiveness.

Young males similarly face difficulties with negative perceptions of their own physical appearance. A significant number of individuals encounter comparable challenges to women, such as issues pertaining to weight and bodily composition. Nevertheless, it is not uncommon for adolescent males to prioritize their muscular development. In contrast to women, the male body is not regarded as an object of consumption by others; rather, it embodies the concept of masculinity. Adolescent males frequently experience the compulsion to cultivate significant muscularity as a means to demonstrate their physical prowess and virility. Furthermore, they commonly harbor insecurities regarding their stature, an attribute over which they have little influence.

Insignificant Entity, Vast Aquatic Environment

Young individuals may often experience a sense of being engulfed by the vastness of the world. This sensation instigates sentiments of insignificance, powerlessness, and inefficacy. Many adolescents do not encounter these emotions until they transition into adulthood, nonetheless, it remains conceivable that individuals of a younger age may undergo what is commonly referred to as an "existential crisis." During this phase, individuals grapple with profound contemplations regarding the nature and purpose of existence. Inquiries such as "what is the underlying meaning or objective of my existence?" When questioning "what truly holds significance in life," the inability to find satisfactory answers poses a formidable risk to an individual's self-esteem.

Unrealistic Goals

When individuals encounter internal or external pressures, including influence from figures of authority or their peers, certain individuals may develop excessively high expectations for themselves in regards to accomplishments such as social standing and extracurricular activities. Individuals who may be encountering challenges in their academic pursuits may hold the belief that they must consistently achieve perfect grades, whereas those who excel academically may attempt to undertake a multitude of extracurricular involvements, anticipating similar levels of success. Individuals who aspire to gain popularity may experience a preoccupation with seeking widespread approval and harboring concerns over potential disapproval, despite the unattainability of universal likability, regardless of one's identity. It remains an inherent impossibility to satisfy the preferences of every individual. The undeniable occurrence of failure in these impractical objectives instills a sense of inadequacy in individuals.

Previous Bad Choices

Individuals frequently find themselves trapped in a cyclical pattern of decision-making and behavior as a result of entrenched habits. This could be attributed to this individual's lack of attentiveness during school, previous shortcomings in friendship, or engagement in hazardous activities such as drug consumption or reckless behavior. They could develop the perception that they inherently possess the characteristic of consistently exhibiting such behavior. Frequently, individuals may develop aversion towards themselves as a result of their regrettable choices in the past, leading them to doubt their capacity to make positive changes in their lives at present. Consequently, they feel disinclined to make any attempts to initiate transformation. Consequently, they persist in making choices that further perpetuate their negative self-perception.

The Beneficial Impact Of Goal Setting On Psychological Well-Being

Establishing objectives can assist individuals in achieving the desired lifestyle. It can provide you with clarity and guidance. This chapter provides an overview of the benefits associated with establishing objectives for the enhancement of one's overall state of wellness. Furthermore, this discourse examines how leveraging your personal strengths can effectively contribute to establishing and attaining objectives.

Sorrow and optimism "

Goals provide individuals with a sense of direction and anticipation for the future. Your life possesses an inherent purpose, fostering a deep sense of hope and optimism within you. Regardless of whether your objectives are short-term or long-term, you are providing yourself with a purpose for rising each morning.

The correlation between hope and goal setting operates in a reciprocal manner. Considering and strategizing about your objectives can enhance a sense of hope and optimism. This positive outlook can subsequently enhance your capacity to accomplish your objectives.

It will further facilitate your strategizing of additional objectives in the future. An individual possessing optimism has the capacity to articulate and establish their objectives, discern the means to attain them, and exhibit the determination to succeed. In addition, hope can assist an individual in navigating any complexities and persevering in the face of adversity.

Taking control

If you establish and attain daily objectives, this will result in notable goal achievements by the conclusion of the year. And it is entirely your own undertaking. Individuals in the Harrou community actively assume responsibility for their lives, rather than passively navigating or allowing external forces to dictate their choices. Acknowledge the sensation of authority and empowerment as you establish and subsequently achieve your objectives.

Consider a situation where you are faced with an unalterable work deadline. Nevertheless, what if you were to proactively choose to meet that deadline in advance? Alternatively, if you possess a tendency to consistently exceed time limits while conjuring excuses, it is imperative that you reverse this pattern and diligently strive to meet the designated deadline.

Acknowledge the extent of your capabilities. Even a change in one's demeanor can engender a sense of mastery. Acquiring the ability to surmount obstacles and cultivating a more constructive mindset towards circumstances beyond one's control significantly enhances confidence.

Flow experience

By establishing regular and meaningful objectives, you position yourself to encounter a greater number of flow experiences. A flow experience entails the complete immersion of one's conscious awareness into a specific activity.

Considerations of time and other requirements (such as hunger) are disregarded. Positive psychologists generally concur that individuals tend to experience greater happiness as the number of flow experiences they have increases. Objectives provide us with a tangible focus that fosters active engagement, which is a vital element in achieving a state of flow.

In order to attain this condition, it is imperative to possess a distinct purpose. It is evident that establishing clear objectives is a favorable initial step. Also, you will want to choose a goal that is challenging for you, but is not out of your depth. If the task lacks sufficient challenge, it is highly probable that one will experience feelings of ennui.

It is advisable to periodically reassess your objectives in order to maintain your motivation. In addition, it is advisable to regularly seek feedback in order to maintain awareness of your performance. Seeking assistance from individuals can prove to be a favorable course of action; alternatively, ensure that you monitor your progress through some means.

Goals and the state of flow demonstrate a positive correlation. By establishing objectives, we amplify the probability of attaining a state of flow. Through the phenomenon of flow, we enhance our likelihood of attaining our objectives.

General wellbeing

Establishing objectives in our existence is beneficial for our overall health and welfare. It presents us with an opportunity to embark on a voyage from which we can derive valuable knowledge and pleasure. It aids individuals in recognizing their competencies, conferring a sense of purpose to their life, and fostering a heightened sense of optimism. As a result, it has the potential to alleviate stress and mitigate the likelihood of developing depression. Engaging in objective-oriented assignments fosters concentration and augments one's sense of contentment.

Objective establishment and leveraging your capabilities

When establishing and pursuing your objectives, it is advisable to contemplate the ways in which one can leverage their inherent strengths to effectively accomplish their goals. It is worthwhile to identify one's primary strengths, as these effortlessly-utilized abilities serve as powerful motivators.

Kindly contemplate the ways in which the subsequent competencies might support you in formulating your objectives:

Inquisitiveness, ingenuity, and a passion for knowledge may facilitate your brainstorming process. This can prove advantageous when contemplating which objectives to establish, determining the strategies to employ in their attainment, and devising approaches to overcome potential challenges.

Courageousness can assist you in pursuing those significant aspirations that you have not yet managed to initiate. This particular attribute will empower you to take action, despite any reservations or uncertainties you may have. If one possesses unwavering perseverance, they are certain to accomplish the goals they have established for themselves.

Possessing a comedic aptitude will afford you the ability to find amusement even in unfortunate circumstances, as you perceive the more lighthearted aspects of existence.

Exercising prudence can assist you in formulating appropriate and enduring objectives, as it enables you to carefully assess the compatibility of your current ambitions with your future aspirations. Maintaining authenticity entails unwavering loyalty to one's true self when establishing personal objectives. It guarantees that you are undertaking these actions for your own benefit rather than to satisfy the expectations of others.

One alternative way to express the same idea in a formal tone could be: "An additional approach to harnessing personal strengths during goal-setting is to establish a dedicated objective aimed at cultivating a specific strength." For example, one may aspire to cultivate greater kindness by opting to engage in volunteer work at an organization that serves individuals in need.

In a formal tone, you could say: "In lieu of that, you may consider utilizing goal setting as a means to cultivate a specific aptitude, even if the said aptitude is not the primary objective." For example, your objective is to compose a novel. Nevertheless, while progressing, you opt to demonstrate your gratitude and hence make a deliberate endeavor to recognize those individuals who aided you in your pursuit of your goal. Regardless of the objectives you establish for yourself, derive pleasure from the process and reflect on the ways in which they are advantageous to you throughout your journey.

Enhancing Self-Perception

Strategy 2

The initial approach outlined in this section entails assuming responsibility for one's own well-being. Upon waking in the morning, I encourage you to embody self-affirmation by greeting your own reflection with a cheerful smile. If you are unable to conjure any positive thoughts, endeavor to take a moment to introspect and envision a desirable scenario. The concept you are attempting to depict pertains to a specific day within your lifetime during which you experienced profound happiness. It can transpire at any given juncture in your lifespan, and I implore you to employ this visual representation whenever you experience pessimistic sentiments throughout the ensuing week. Rather than letting negative thoughts linger in your mind, when faced with adversity, envision a state of happiness and consciously avoid dwelling on pessimistic aspects.

Gaze upon your reflection in the mirror, ponder upon a pleasant notion, and then proceed to ready yourself for the day ahead. Take care of yourself. Ensure that you present yourself in an aesthetically pleasing manner by meticulously observing your appearance in a full-length mirror prior to departing from your residence. It is advisable to don comfortable footwear as it enhances stability and ensures a more confident stride. Please don attire that is comfortably fitted yet appropriate for the activities you have planned for the day. Welcome the world with a pleasant countenance – and that encompasses even individuals you encounter who typically evoke negative emotions about your self-worth. Acquiring mastery may require a substantial investment of time, but the cultivation of a positive mindset serves as a catalyst for significant life improvement. When positivity emanates from within oneself, the subsequent outcomes will undoubtedly be highly favorable.

It is imperative that you take care of yourself, as it is your personal duty. It is imperative that you consume appropriate nutrition. It is imperative that you obtain the appropriate quantity of sleep. These are matters of basic logic, however, how about the degree of optimism and motivation you cultivate within yourself? It is highly probable that you underestimate your accomplishments in life, and this is a significant error. It is imperative that you overcome the belief that you do not deserve to invest time in self-care and recognize that prioritizing yourself is paramount in your life. One would not acquire confidence and self-esteem by prioritizing others over oneself.

Strategy number three – the active engagement of volunteers

While you may not have prior familiarity with engaging in volunteer work, genuine volunteering entails providing assistance without seeking validation or approval from others. It pertains to extending assistance without any ulterior motives or expectations of reciprocity. This exemplifies genuine volunteerism and serves to enhance one's sense of self-worth, as it is driven purely by altruistic intentions. You are not actively pursuing validation. You are merely engaging in this action due to your inherent kindness. Whether that entails preparing a cake for a solitary neighbor or extending an offer to accompany a friend's canine companion for a stroll, kindly offer your assistance to others and cultivate a daily routine of generosity. An excellent beginning would be to seek out a nearby animal shelter that requires assistance, as approval from animals is not forthcoming. What they will provide to you is a profound sense of accomplishment that necessitates no validation from others. In a similar fashion, one may choose to pay visits to hospitalized individuals lacking company, engage in voluntary work at a hospital shop, offer assistance within their local place of worship, or contribute their efforts to serving soup at a nearby charitable soup kitchen. It is evident that you are acting out of altruistic intentions and do not require validation from others. However, your actions serve to reinforce your inherent worth as an individual.

The efficacy of volunteerism lies in its holistic nature, extending beyond mere acts of giving. The primary focus lies in selflessly offering without any anticipation or requirement of acknowledgment. When evaluating the scenario where a parent consistently reinforces to their child that the child has not met the expectations set by the parent, the child develops a sense of inadequacy as they mature. Nevertheless, upon a careful evaluation of this scenario, it becomes evident that the parent has indeed provided considerable resources to the child, albeit with certain conditions attached. Whenever you engage in that behavior, you consistently find yourself dissatisfied with the outcomes. In the act of volunteering, one bestows their contributions without any associated conditions or obligations. It is possible that somebody may express appreciation, but it is also possible that they may not. When engaging in voluntary activities, the focus does not rest solely on achieving specific outcomes. It pertains to offering without harboring any expectations of reciprocation. Once you acquire the capacity to accomplish that, you will observe a rapid transformation within yourself. You find yourself expressing gratitude for your true identity. One starts to recognize one's own value and cultivates self-confidence, which should be the essence of engaging in volunteer work. One does not engage in self-praise or anticipate expressions of gratitude, as the received appreciation comes in humble forms. You are able to experience a sense of accomplishment, which is easily achieved in this manner.

Individuals who possess challenges with their self-esteem consistently seek validation from others. They are uncertain about their position or stability in life. Volunteering, to some extent, provides a broader understanding of this matter. The canine companion entrusted to your care during the walk earlier today might not have expressed gratitude, but it is plausible that you derived satisfaction from their presence, harboring the knowledge that your contribution facilitated the fulfillment of crucial tasks for a benevolent organization. If you assist a child in their academic assignments, it is incumbent upon you to do so with the intention of fostering the child's growth and aptitude in the domain of education. One engages in the act not driven by personal expectations, but by a recognition of the potential benefits that the child may derive from it.

Engaging in voluntary work also fosters a sense of worth and direction in one's life, something that individuals facing self-esteem challenges often overlook as they turn their focus inward. You will not have the opportunity to engage in that activity when you commit to volunteering. Please proceed to bake a cake for your adjacent resident. Rectify their garden gate solely based on your personal desire. If they inquire about the amount owed, kindly convey your sincere pleasure in providing the service without charge.

Effective Practices For Enhancing One's Self-Esteem

What steps can I take to cultivate and enhance my self-esteem?

In order to enhance your self-esteem, it is imperative to confront and modify the detrimental beliefs you hold regarding your own self. While you may perceive this task as arduous, rest assured that there are numerous alternative strategies at your disposal that can assist you in overcoming it.

Engage in activities that bring you pleasure.

Partaking in activities that bring you pleasure and where you excel can contribute to enhancing your spirits and bolstering your self-assurance. You can accomplish this objective by implementing incentives in the form of rewards for productivity such as complimentary services, empathy, or leisurely pursuits.

Work

Employment can bestow individual character, camaraderie, a steadfast routine, and compensation. A limited number of individuals thrive in a busy environment and value the opportunity to work towards achieving their goals. Alternative phrasing in a formal tone: "Some individuals perceive work as an undesirable obligation or responsibility when it comes to unpaid voluntary positions." No matter what endeavors you undertake, it is paramount that you harbor a sense of unwavering resolve and support in your professional journey, ensuring that the alignment of your professional and personal life is attuned to your individual needs and desires.

Pastime activities

This could encompass a variety of activities, ranging from acquiring a new linguistic skill to vocalization or engaging in formal instruction in the field of visual arts. Reflect upon areas where you perceive inherent qualities or endeavors that have long piqued your interest. Seek out exercises that provide a manageable level of challenge, enabling you to experience a sense of achievement while also bolstering your morale. Online platforms, academic repositories, and institutions of higher learning should provide information pertaining to local clubs and classes that you may express an interest in attending. The act of crafting or creating things engenders a growing sense of self-assurance within me. Upon observing my own creations and experiencing a favorable impression of them, I consequently derive a sense of self-satisfaction, as I perceive this as a significant realization of my exceptional aptitude.

Strive to establish constructive relationships

Make an effort to engage with individuals who will not subject you to excessive scrutiny, and with whom you feel prepared to engage in conversations regarding your emotions. By surrounding yourself with individuals who exhibit a constructive and unwavering demeanor, you are likely to experience an enhanced sense of self-worth and a heightened level of determination. As a result, should one consistently display care and steadiness towards others, it is inevitable that they will elicit a favorable response. This will empower you to experience a sense of self-worth and positively influence the perception of others towards you.

If you suffer from low self-esteem, there may be individuals in close proximity who reinforce the negative beliefs and assumptions that you harbor. It is critical to point out these individuals and make a move to stop them from doing this, maybe by becoming more self-assured or by restricting the amount of time, you interact with them.

Develop strategies for effectively expressing oneself assertively.

Exhibiting assertiveness indicates that you hold yourself and others in high regard, and communicate with mutual respect. It will aid you in establishing explicit boundaries. The subsequent factors will facilitate the enhancement of your assertive behavior:

• Give due attention to both your verbal and non-verbal communication, ensuring that you project openness and confidence.

• Endeavor to articulate your emotions if you have been unsettled – restrain yourself until you regain composure and elucidate clearly your state of mind.

• Decline irrational requests.

• Kindly inform your peers or superiors in a courteous manner if you require extra time or assistance with challenging assignments.

- Try to talk in the first individual where it is applicable – for example 'When you speak to me like that, I feel… '. This provides you with the opportunity to express your requirements without appearing assertive or apprehensive.

Developing assertiveness can be a challenging skill to acquire, necessitating the practice of speaking in front of a reflective surface or conversing with a trusted individual. Many educational institutions catering to adults, such as schools and universities, also provide courses on assertiveness. Furthermore, numerous self-improvement manuals containing practical exercises and tips are readily available for purchase or utilization through online platforms.

Ensure that you attend to your physical welfare.

Attending to your physical well-being can enhance your emotional state and overall sense of worth, while also bolstering your self-perception.

Engaging in physical activities enhances individuals' sense of well-being and self-perception. Engaging in physical activity releases endorphins, which are known as "feel-good" hormones that have the potential to enhance your mental well-being, particularly when performed in an outdoor setting.

Rest

The lack of adequate rest can lead to an inaccurate representation of negative emotions, implying a potential decrease in confidence. Therefore, it is imperative to prioritize obtaining sufficient rest.

Diet

Consuming a nutritionally balanced diet at regular intervals, accompanied by an ample intake of water and vegetables, will contribute to an enhanced sense of wellbeing and increased happiness. Reducing or abstaining from alcohol intake and refraining from the use of tobacco and illicit substances can also contribute to enhancing your overall well-being.

Establish a personal objective

If you establish objectives for yourself and make diligent efforts to attain them, you will experience a sense of fulfillment and self-appreciation upon reaching your goals, leading to a gradual increase in self-confidence and positivity.

Make sure that the goals you set for yourself are attainable and aligned with a practical outlook. It may not be imperative for it to be a substantial matter, but it should possess significance to you. As an example, you have the option of drafting a letter to your local newspaper or embarking on regular attendance at an exercise class.

Determine effective strategies to identify and confront negative beliefs

Enhancing your self-esteem may also unveil the underlying origins and negative perceptions you hold about yourself. This process may be intricate, therefore it is imperative to allocate sufficient time and consider enlisting the assistance of a companion or collaborator. If you are experiencing distress, it could be beneficial to seek guidance from a professional advisor to facilitate this process. It would prove advantageous to document any pertinent information and inquiries. For instance, doing so could facilitate the organization and coherence of one's thoughts.

• What do you perceive as your areas of weakness or shortcomings?

• What negative perceptions do you believe others hold towards you?

• In brief, how would you describe yourself using the term 'I am...'?

• At what point did these sensations first manifest for you?

• Could you possibly identify a specific encounter or event that may have contributed to this inclination?

- Do you find that you often harbor consistent negative thoughts?

It could also prove valuable to maintain a written log or diary of ideas over the course of several weeks. Document the specific details pertaining to the circumstances, your emotional state, and your analysis of the fundamental belief.

Concentrate on positive things. If one experiences a lack of self-esteem, it may require consistent effort to acclimate oneself to adopting a more positive self-perception. One possible approach to accomplishing this objective involves compiling a series of attributes that you appreciate about yourself. You have the option to include:

- Aspects of your personality

- Aspects pertaining to one's appearance
- Matters concerning one's physical attributes • Factors related to personal aesthetics • Considerations regarding one's visual presentation • Elements pertaining to one's outward appearance

- Actions that you undertake • Activities that you engage in • Tasks that you perform • Behaviors that you exhibit

- Developed skills.

Please allow yourself ample time to identify and compile a comprehensive list of 50 distinct elements, without concern for the duration it may take to complete this task. Retain this list and examine a distinct item from it on a daily basis. In the event that you are experiencing negative emotions or experiencing stress in anticipation of an upcoming event, such as a professional networking event, you can effectively employ this occasion as an opportunity to remind yourself of your positive attributes. If you encounter difficulty in brainstorming a comprehensive inventory of valuable belongings, you may seek assistance from a collaborator or a confidant to facilitate your initial efforts.

This can also aid in perceiving how others may hold a greater esteem for you than you hold for yourself. An alternative approach entails documenting a minimum of three positive occurrences or personal achievements from the day prior to taking rest. Some individuals also hold the belief that it is conducive to retain possessions, such as photographs or letters, that foster self-affinity.

Engage in strategies centered around mindfulness "

Mindfulness is a practice that entails directing attention to the present moment, employing techniques such as meditation, deep breathing, and yoga. It has been demonstrated to aid individuals in developing heightened awareness of their thoughts and emotions, enabling them to effectively manage and regulate them rather than being overwhelmed by them.

How can family members and close friends provide support?

When acquaintances with individuals exhibiting low self-esteem are encountered, a range of strategic alternatives can be pursued.

Exhibit to them your genuine concern - assure them of your unwavering support and regard for their well-being. One may effectively convey their emotions to others by displaying tenderness, actively listening, or devoting quality time to their presence.

Assist individuals in recollecting the positive aspects - although one cannot alter individuals' negative perception of themselves, it is possible to contribute towards challenging this perspective by aiding them in recalling their noteworthy accomplishments, such as significant achievements or positive contributions they have made.

Refrain from assigning blame to others – individuals with diminished self-esteem often attribute negative experiences to themselves, including mental health issues. Assure them that this is not their fault and refrain from instructing them to 'compose themselves.'

It is advisable to display perseverance, as instances of low self-esteem typically manifest after prolonged periods. Altering an individual's self-evaluation necessitates a considerable duration, and they might require recurrent reassurance.

Communicate to them that experiencing occasional distress is permissible, as it is uncommon for individuals to perpetually experience joy and motivation. Moreover, emphasize the significance of not feeling obligated to fulfill irrational expectations.

Exhibit support – when your associate or family member engages in a self-enhancement program or seeks guidance from a counselor, demonstrate support and encouragement. One could also extend substantial assistance, such as offering childcare services in order to enable their attendance at meetings.

Facilitate their search for appropriate treatment - if you have concerns about the impact of low self-esteem on their psychological well-being, encourage your companion or relative to actively pursue suitable therapeutic options.

Self-improvement resources

Take into consideration these key strategies to facilitate the development of your self-confidence.

• Engage in physical activities that you find enjoyable.

• Allocate time to engage with individuals who are constructive and exhibit stability.

• Display a willingness to assist and accommodate others.

• It is advisable to refrain from making comparisons with other individuals. • Endeavor to avoid drawing comparisons between yourself and other individuals.
• It is recommended that you abstain

from engaging in comparisons with other individuals.

• Endeavor to engage in consistent physical activity, consume a nutritious diet, and prioritize sufficient sleep.

• Exude assertiveness – do not afford individuals the opportunity to disregard you or disrespect you.

• Utilize resources such as self-improvement literature and online platforms to cultivate a nurturing skill set, including traits like assertiveness or mindfulness.

• Develop the ability to question and contest your negative beliefs.

• Recognize and acknowledge your commendable attributes and areas in which you excel. • Take stock of your positive traits and accomplishments.

• Develop the practice of recollecting and articulating affirmative statements about oneself.

Why is Self-Esteem of paramount importance?

Self-esteem refers to the personal convictions individuals hold regarding their own intrinsic value and worth. It is also rooted in the subjective emotional responses that individuals experience, which can range from feelings of significance to feelings of disgrace. Self-esteem is crucial as it profoundly shapes the decision-making and behavioral choices of individuals. Self-esteem plays a motivating role by significantly enhancing the likelihood that individuals will attend to their own needs and strive towards realizing their full potential. Individuals possessing high levels of self-esteem are more inclined to prioritize self-care and strive towards the attainment of personal goals and desires. Generally, individuals who possess lower levels of self-esteem tend to view themselves as unworthy of positive outcomes or capable of achieving them. Consequently, they may overlook important matters and exhibit lower levels of persistence and adaptability when faced with challenges. Individuals with higher levels of self-esteem possess distinct objectives, but they generally exhibit a diminished inclination to actively pursue and achieve these aims.

Self-confidence can be considered an abstract concept to some extent, making it difficult for individuals lacking it to truly comprehend its essence and significance. An avenue for individuals with diminished self-esteem to cultivate an understanding of elevated self-esteem is to ponder their sentiments towards aspects in their lives that they value. For instance, it is evident that a considerable number of individuals have a fondness for automobiles. Due to the importance of vehicles to these individuals, they give careful consideration to their automobiles. They exercise prudent discernment regarding the selection of parking locations, the frequency of vehicle maintenance, and their driving habits. They may enhance the vehicle and subsequently showcase it to others with a sense of satisfaction. Self-esteem, in essence, involves the nurturing, appreciation, and satisfaction one finds in oneself. When children embrace these attributes, they assume a position of significance and worth, demonstrating commendable self-care. They exercise astute discernment in evaluating themselves, thereby enhancing their value rather than diminishing it.

What Does This Book Contain And Who Should Engage With Its Contents?

It would be advantageous to have a clear understanding of the contents covered in the book, thus ensuring that you have selected the most suitable choice, especially if you remain undecided about its relevance to you. It is highly probable that if you are perusing this text and can establish a connection to the content thus far, you would possess an inclination to proceed further. But just to clarify. "This book caters to individuals who:

• Seek to enhance their self-assurance and self-esteem.

• Aspire to devote substantial attention to their personal well-being, aiming to cultivate greater contentment and self-affection.

- Desire to awaken with self-acceptance and contentment.

- Aspire to possess an influential presence and exhibit genuine authenticity.

- Display a willingness to dedicate time and effort consistently in order to assist themselves.

- Acknowledge that outcomes are not achieved instantaneously.

- Display a willingness to initiate requests for assistance and enhance their level of transparency.

- Are amenable to the use of profanity. In my prior literary works, I refrained from articulating profanities despite my desire to do so.

Sound like you? Excellent :) I knew you were an action-taker kind of person.

In the course of the book, I consistently convey my personal anecdotes alongside a few anecdotes unrelated to my own experiences. The narratives pertaining to other individuals do not feature actual acquaintances of mine; instead, I have amalgamated anecdotes from individuals within my personal circle and fabricated the corresponding identities. In addition, I have proposed measures to assist you. I would advise against overwhelming oneself by undertaking an excessive number of tasks described in the book. Kindly select a handful and endeavor to incorporate them. Record your emotions in a journal or diary. Additionally, I recommend thoroughly reviewing the book multiple times at your leisure, as this will aid in better retention of the material.

I have observed that through multiple readings, typically ranging between five to ten times, I have acquired and retained a significant amount of knowledge from the books.

Altering Your Mindset, Transforming Your Life

This quote, attributed to Wayne Dyer, is of profound significance.

To effect a transformation in your thoughts, it is imperative that you make a deliberate and conscious decision to embrace change. This may necessitate endeavoring and implementing deliberate strategies, however, subsequent actions are significantly influenced by cognitive processes. Therefore, it is imperative to allocate time for the reprogramming of one's beliefs and thoughts. It is imperative to allocate time for cultivating a mindset that fosters self-esteem and confidence.

On certain occasions, when confronted with a challenge that extends beyond my customary boundaries, I experience a sensation of unease akin to any typical human being. Abstain from engaging in such actions" or "Multiple internal dialogues discouraging the act and presenting unfavorable justifications. I am aware, nevertheless, that by undertaking the action I am apprehensive about, I will further augment my self-assurance. That unequivocally represents my mission, and I fervently desire for it to align with yours.

How can one cultivate a mindset of self-esteem and confidence through training?

Allow us to extend our warmest greetings as we embark on the journey that lies within the remaining pages of this book.... I will serve as your personal trainer in enhancing self-esteem and confidence throughout the course of this read.

However, a transformative effect on your life can only be achieved through proactive implementation.

Therapeutic Interventions And Psychosocial Support - Stage 2

Secondly, the implementation of therapy and counseling should be considered.

The following step in constructing or reconstructing one's self-esteem involves the involvement of a therapist. Not every individual experiencing low self-esteem will necessarily require the assistance of a therapist. However, the factors that were deliberated upon in chapter 1 may potentially result in the necessity for professional intervention.

"The Responsibilities of the Therapist

The therapist's function in addressing low self-esteem is both instructional and remedial. A potential strategy to enhance one's self-esteem or conquer a state of diminished self-esteem, if necessary, entails acquiring new coping mechanisms. Individuals of all walks of life are confronted with various challenges, irrespective of their fortitude, as even the most self-assured individuals encounter their fair share of concerns.

Not all individuals seeking to enhance their self-esteem require the assistance of a therapist, however, those who do find themselves in need of additional support may greatly benefit from their expertise and guidance. The objective they pursue does not involve the attainment of elevated self-esteem for the client, as the true antithesis of diminished self-esteem lies in embracing oneself and fostering inner assurance. The therapist will endeavor to assist the client in attaining a state of constructive self-acknowledgment.

This poses a significant obstacle for both the therapist and the client, as the phenomenon of decreased self-assurance, commonly referred to as low self-esteem, typically emerges and persists throughout an individual's lifespan. It will not be resolved expeditiously.

Is it necessary for me to seek the guidance of a therapist?

What criteria should be taken into consideration to determine if undertaking this course of action is suitable for oneself and whether the involvement of a therapist is necessary? Low self-esteem is widely regarded as a maladaptive condition by numerous psychologists. Regardless of the nature of the disorder or dysfunction presented by a client, a prevalent underlying factor typically involves diminished self-esteem. Numerous contemporary challenges find resolution through the attainment of self-acceptance and the eradication of diminished self-esteem.

Each person bears the responsibility of determining whether their specific concerns, such as depression, relationship difficulties, or anxiety and panic attacks, warrant seeking assistance from a qualified therapist.

We will now examine several therapeutic approaches that have been proven efficacious in addressing individuals experiencing challenges with low self-esteem.

Solution Focused Therapy

Solution-focused therapy, also known as solution-focused brief therapy (SFBT), derives its name from its core focus on the desired outcome sought by the therapist in the sessions, as opposed to fixating on the symptoms or manifestations of low self-esteem. This therapy follows a goal-centric approach wherein the emphasis lies on achieving desired outcomes rather than the procedural aspects.

The primary objective of this research is to address the ramifications of existing and potential low self-esteem, with the aim of attaining the desired outcome of self-acceptance. The scholars do not place any emphasis on past events and their associated implications. The therapist shall collaborate with the client to envision a future devoid of diminished self-worth, followed by developing a comprehensive set of objectives that will guide the individual towards the desired future state.

After defining their desired vision for the future, the therapist will collaborate with the client in identifying the existing resources and competencies that will enable them to achieve that vision.

The therapist will demonstrate empathy towards the client and collaborate with them to facilitate the client's independent exploration of effective techniques, ultimately encouraging them to acknowledge and commemorate their achievements. The therapist employs distinct inquiries to facilitate the client in identifying their personal strengths. Should the therapist pose a query that illuminates to the client their existing coping mechanisms for addressing challenges that they perceive as inadequacies, it could potentially result in a boost in their sense of self-worth.

Cognitive-Behavioral Therapy

Cognitive-behavioral therapy is an alternative form of therapy that has proven efficacy in enhancing individuals' self-confidence and self-esteem. The objective of this therapy is to assist patients in refraining from engaging in self-criticism that may be unjust or unwarranted. The client is requested to disclose during every session the most recent instance in which they engaged in self-criticism and the underlying rationale behind it. The session is subsequently designed to demonstrate to the client that the criticism is unjust.

Simultaneously, this therapeutic approach will illuminate the client's actual errors, shortcomings, and vulnerabilities while assisting them in perceiving these factors as typical occurrences. All individuals are prone to making errors and exhibiting weaknesses and shortcomings. The objective is to aid the client in perceiving these matters as commonplace and refrain from engaging in self-criticism regarding them. Subsequently, individuals can also develop the capacity to acknowledge their own positive accomplishments and graciously receive expressions of admiration.

Subsequently, it is necessary for the therapist to impart to their client the necessary proficiencies for achieving success and cultivating self-acceptance.

Summary and Action Plan

The therapist's responsibility lies in facilitating the transition of the client from a state of diminished self-assurance to a state of heightened self-assurance. They aid in the identification of the areas requiring assistance most urgently. Presented below are several strategies that can assist you in supporting yourself.

- Reflect on one daily occurrence in which you experienced a sense of inadequacy or perceived yourself as being inferior to others. Direct your focus towards the ideological framework you employ to evaluate your own actions in this particular situation. What internal dialogues or self-reflections shape your perception of failure in that particular circumstance? Write it all down. Please refrain from passing judgment on your thoughts or verbal expressions in these particular circumstances - simply record them with complete honesty.

- Perform a weekly analysis of your written reflections on each situation and critically examine any negative or erroneous thoughts that you may be conveying. Are you being logical? Do your thoughts and internal dialogue derive from factual information or a propensity towards negativity? Employ unvarnished candor when evaluating yourself. Please distribute this information to a single individual whose judgment you confidently rely on, and duly factor in their insights. Were they of the opinion that you lacked proficiency, or were they under the impression that you were expressing negativity and veering away from verifiable facts?

• Attempt to counteract and overcome your own pessimistic thought patterns. Take into account that your initial analysis of the situation may not be the sole perspective from which it can be examined. What alternative perspective can be adopted to perceive the same situation in a more optimistic light?

• Surround yourself exclusively with individuals who offer support and foster a positive environment. Do not allow external influences to instill negative thoughts or beliefs within oneself.

• Take responsibility for yourself. If you approach this task with sincerity, you will gradually experience a sense of empowerment over your own existence, fostering an eventual embrace of your true self. Remind yourself on a daily basis about your personal responsibility in striving towards the realization of your own aspirations. It is incumbent upon you to assume responsibility for the choices that you make. It is incumbent upon you to assume accountability for your own beliefs and actions.

Effective Strategies For Enhancing Positivity

7 Excellent Ways to Increase Your Positivity

1. Look for the Companionship of Individuals with a Positive Outlook

The individuals with whom you choose to associate can exert a substantial influence over one's mental state. It is widely acknowledged within the field of psychology that one's thoughts and behavior are influenced by the amalgamation of the personalities of the five individuals with whom they associate most frequently. These 'five individuals' can consist of tangible individuals such as acquaintances, relatives, colleagues... or intangible sources of influence such as literature, television, online platforms, printed media, and so forth.

Your cognitive faculties demonstrate considerable receptivity. It demonstrates rapid learning capabilities! These influences have the potential to exert highly favorable or highly detrimental effects upon you. Continuous exposure to individuals with negative dispositions may invariably undermine one's ability to experience joy or cultivate self-assurance. If one consistently associates with friends who consistently express dissatisfaction and grievances, it is likely that one will also adopt a tendency to frequently complain.

2. Engage in the consumption of literary works, visual media, and audio recordings authored by individuals whom you hold in high regard.

Recently, we deliberated on the notion that it would be prudent to allocate a majority of our time in the presence of individuals who exude positivity and exemplify triumph. However, in the event that our present social circle lacks individuals of such nature, what course of action should we pursue? What course of action should we pursue?

Allow me to present you with a favorable development - the power of positive influence does not necessarily depend on the physical presence of individuals. It may encompass their literary works, audio recordings, visual media, motion pictures, musical compositions... It all counts. Now, you are no longer justified in claiming, 'I lack the resources to personally encounter all those accomplished individuals'.

Seek out individuals whom you hold in high regard and engage with their literary works, video presentations, and audio recordings... You will unconsciously assimilate their thought processes and actions.

Peruse their literary works and engage with their audiovisual content...

All aspects contribute to the transformation of our mindset towards a positive orientation.

Well-written self-help books and autobiographies possess the capacity to greatly aid individuals in their personal development. An individual who has encountered numerous difficulties throughout their lifetime opts to document all that acquired wisdom in a comprehensible book... This epitomizes a genuine prospect. One can acquire the knowledge they attained and apply it in analogous circumstances.

Engaging in literary pursuits enhances one's creative faculties, broadens one's intellectual horizons, and reveals the boundless possibilities that exist within our realm. Through the act of reading, individuals are able to cultivate a fresh vantage point on familiar concepts or gain insight into the diverse consequences that can arise from various courses of action. Books are beyond imagination. It resembles an expansive network of interconnected threads, where one continuously establishes connections to existing knowledge as well as newly acquired information, thereby formulating novel solutions and responses.

As you persist in immersing yourself in uplifting influences, you will discern a proclivity towards cultivating positive thoughts throughout the course of your day.

3. Positive Self-Talk

Engaging in constructive self-affirmation is essential for achieving success. If one is able to modify the inner voice, one can attain limitless capabilities.

Numerous studies have provided empirical evidence that the human brain possesses the remarkable capacity to undergo substantial alterations throughout the later stages of adulthood. The term used to describe this phenomenon is known as "neuroplasticity."

Each and every thought that arises within our minds, whether it be a conscious or subconscious thought, undergoes translation into electrical impulses. These impulses, in turn, exert influence over the emotions we experience, the verbal expressions we articulate, and the behaviors we engage in.

Our cognitive processes are shaped through the programming of our mind by means of our internal dialogues.

It constitutes the medium of cognitive communication.

Therefore, engaging in self-dialogue also presents an occasion to challenge and revise our previous adverse conditioning through the practice of repetition.

Please provide guidance on the appropriate steps to undertake. By leveraging the technique of self-dialogue, how can we modify the ceaseless internal discourse occurring within our minds?

The solution is straightforward: employing the appropriate language.

Employing affirmative and contemporaneous declarations, such as "I am..." or "at present, I acknowledge..." or "I am transitioning...", underscores the ongoing transformations taking place in the current instant. In the not too distant future. As an illustration, consider uttering the phrase, "I intend to cultivate virtuous qualities," and pay attention to the sensations it elicits.

Not very inspiring, eh?

Kindly express the statement, "I possess moral integrity."

How did that feel?

One can achieve profound rewiring of the brain through the consistent application of positive, present-tense affirmations on a daily basis. Replace the outdated and detrimental internal dialogue with a constructive alternative, and engage in its repetition during any available moments of leisure.

A selection of self-affirmations that particularly resonate with me is:

"I am enough."

I am capable of completing the task. I possess the ability to accomplish it. I have the proficiency required to execute the task. I am competent in undertaking the task. I am qualified to handle the assignment.

The presence of God is perpetual in my life." "I am constantly accompanied by the divine." "The eternal presence of God never leaves my side." "I am always within the embrace of the divine."

I have emerged as the victorious individual.

Today belongs to me."

I am entitled to the highest quality and I consistently strive for excellence."

"I forgive myself."

I have a profound and unwavering love and acceptance for myself."

I am deserving of love precisely as I am." "I am entitled to receive love as I currently am." "I have inherent value and deserve to be loved as I am."

The act of consistently reiterating these positive self-affirmations not only exerts a substantial, beneficial impact on my own life, but also in the lives of those individuals with whom I choose to share them. You have the option to either embrace these suggestions or devise customized alternatives that align with your specific requirements.

If you plan on generating new affirmations independently, please ensure that they embody positivity and are expressed in the present tense.

Chapter 5

The Significance of Establishing Behavior Patterns to Regulate Emotional Response

Evaluating one's own emotional state is a critical factor in developing emotional intelligence and fostering empathy in a broader context. Certain individuals may possess a perpetual awareness of their emotional states, while others may go extended periods of time without giving it any consideration. Whilst it may be tempting to succumb to the tendency of making sweeping statements regarding individuals who contemplate their actions versus those who do not, this matter is more nuanced than initially perceived.

Individuals who express a tendency to regularly contemplate their emotional experiences can be typified as individuals of a sensitive and empathetic disposition. These individuals possess an inherent inclination to inquire about the emotional well-being of others or to offer support and encouragement upon learning of situations that imply the other person may be facing difficulties. Certain individuals possess an innate ability to discern their own emotional condition, consequently fostering their sensitivity towards the emotional disposition of others.

On the other hand, there are individuals who appear to exhibit a lack of concern for the emotional well-being of others. These individuals exhibit behaviors that indicate a lack of empathetic comprehension or disregard for the emotions of others. In the film Fried Green Tomatoes, a scene unfolds wherein one of the main characters experiences the unfortunate event of having their parking spot usurped by a briefly appearing character, who subsequently proceeds to make a derogatory comment. This appears to be an individual who displays a lack of empathy towards the emotions of others and likely struggles to acknowledge and process their own emotions, including feelings of anger. Individuals of this nature are frequently perceived as deficient in empathetic abilities.

However, the demarcation between individuals who acknowledge their own emotions and those who are perceived not to is not as unequivocal as the individual who has their parking spot illicitly taken and sheds tears, as opposed to the other individual who perpetrates the malicious act and revels in a callously triumphant manner. Certainly, individuals of such nature do exist within our society, and a considerable number of us have indeed encountered them. Films often incline towards the portrayal of exaggerated characters, owing to their time constraints and the necessity to effectively convey a person's essence.

However, it is a fact that individuals who are commonly perceived as being unaware of their emotions or lacking in empathy might not possess the heartlessness that is commonly attributed to them. This topic is under investigation for several purposes, primarily to acquaint you with the notion that the interconnectedness of emotional intelligence and empathy is significant. Acknowledging one's emotions is vital as a personal competency, however, it ought to be complemented by the presence of empathy, the ability to perceive and understand the emotions of others, self-control, and the encompassing set of abilities that comprise emotional intelligence.

Our intention is to emphasize that the utmost importance lies in acknowledging one's own emotions, enabling the ability to subsequently acknowledge the emotions of others. Acknowledging your own emotions is equally crucial in the context of self-regulation, a concept that entails the capacity to cease or redirect one's own maladaptive emotions, as previously mentioned. If one is capable of acknowledging their own emotions but chooses to disregard the emotions of others, prioritizing solely their own thoughts and feelings, it is possible that they are displaying narcissistic tendencies, which greatly differs from the practice of empathy.

We may delve deeper into this aspect by referring back to the illustrative instance from Fried Green Tomatoes. It is evident that the protagonist who experiences agitation and comprehends the cause of her agitation is acknowledging her emotional state. The lack of clarity lies in the precise nature of the situation involving the other character. It is our conjecture that the other character is lacking self-awareness, given their apparent disregard for the emotions of others. There exists a predisposition to amalgamate individuals into a vast amalgamation of "individuals who display indifference towards emotions," a strategy that dilutes the recognition of nuanced differences.

It is conceivable that the character exhibiting inconsiderate behavior is acknowledging his own emotions. Acknowledging one's own emotions does not inevitably indicate a profound consideration for the emotions of others. As previously mentioned, the importance of acknowledging one's own emotions within the framework of emotional intelligence and empathy lies in its ability to foster an understanding of others' emotions, facilitate the display of compassion, and promote empathy. The character displaying a lack of empathy towards others may have experienced internal emotions that influenced her behavior, contrasting with the assumptions made by the observer.

This individual—the motorist who rudely overtakes another driver, appropriates their parking space, and subsequently utters an inhospitable remark—might have been vexed due to their tardiness or jubilant because they had secured a parking spot, thereby alleviating the need to spend an additional 10 minutes searching for an alternative location. These sentiments of fury and ecstasy are entirely legitimate emotional responses. These are identifiable by individuals who actively endeavor to acknowledge their emotions.

The issue at hand pertains to the fact that mere acknowledgment of one's own emotions does not guarantee the manifestation of empathetic behavior towards the emotions experienced by others. A narcissist exhibits sensitivity towards their own emotions and desires, however, this sensitivity does not translate into them embodying kindness, compassion, and care for others. A narcissistic individual exhibits an exclusive focus on their own desires and motivations, displaying blatant indifference towards the emotions and desires of others. An individual who possesses the ability to acknowledge their own emotions but fails to then evaluate, comprehend, and demonstrate empathy towards the emotions of others exhibits narcissistic conduct, which is detrimental and inconsiderate towards those who come into contact with the narcissist.

This differentiation bears significant importance as certain individuals emphasize the recognition and subsequent response to emotions as a pivotal instrument in enhancing emotional intelligence and promoting personal empowerment. However, it is imperative to note that engaging in this pursuit merely serves to rationalize and foster tendencies towards narcissistic behavior. An individual who opts against accommodating their recently injured sibling or child in their residence temporarily, citing inconvenience, might be acknowledging their personal sentiments and acting accordingly, yet they could possibly be encroaching upon narcissistic inclinations.

It is imperative to delve into this narcissistic aspect of emotional recognition, as it represents a behavioral pattern that is not only devoid of empathy, but in outright contradiction to empathy. Through the exhibition of narcissistic behavior, we deplete both our own reserves of empathy as well as that of those around us. We foster a society in which individuals are driven by intense anger, pursuit of self-interest, malice, and the desire for vengeance. The efficacy of empathy and emotional intelligence lies in the capacity to harness emotions for the purpose of establishing meaningful connections with individuals. If individuals prioritize solely their own emotions and exhibit a lack of sensitivity towards the emotions of others, they are not fostering meaningful connections, but rather eroding them.

www.ingramcontent.com/pod-product-compliance
Lightning Source LLC
Chambersburg PA
CBHW050244120526
44590CB00016B/2216